God Helps Martin

God Helps Us

Sometimes I worry about

scare me.

I don't like to think about

God Helps Us

Some things SCARE me. Move the **S** to the end of the word to make a new word.

But God ______ ______ ______ ______ ______ about me.

Shade in the cloud next to each picture that tells about a time when you were afraid.

Circle the cross next to each picture that tells about a time when God helped you.

I Am Trusting You, Lord Jesus

I am trusting You, Lord Jesus,
Trusting only You;
Trusting You for full salvation,
Free and true.

I am trusting You for pardon;
At Your feet I bow,
For Your grace and tender mercy
Trusting now.

I am trusting You for cleansing
In the crimson flood;
Trusting You to make me holy
By Your blood.

I am trusting You to guide me;
You alone shall lead,
Ev'ry day and hour supplying
All my need.

Words to Remember

Trust in the Lord with all your heart. Proverbs 3:5

Draw a picture of yourself.

Luther's Ninety-Five Theses

At the time when Martin Luther became a pastor, the church said that people could buy papers to forgive their sins. One of the people who sold these papers was John Tetzel. Luther did not agree with what John Tetzel was doing. Luther knew from the Bible that Jesus earned the forgiveness for our sins by dying on a cross. Luther wrote ninety-five sentences to tell why he disagreed with what the church was doing. He nailed these sentences on the door of the church on October 31, 1517, for all to see.

Place the sticker of Luther onto the scene.

The Bible Shows Us the Way to Heaven

Use your pencil to follow the path. Then add stickers to show the message of the Bible. The Bible leads us to Jesus, and Jesus is the way to heaven.

Words to Remember

Your word is a lamp to my feet and a light to my path.
Psalm 119:105

I Thank God for the Bible

Dear Jesus, thank You for giving me the Bible so I can know that You love me. Thank You for forgiving me. Here are the names of some of Your children who are forgiven:

Name________________

Name________________

Name________________

Name________________

Your ______ is a ______

to my ______ and a ______

to my ______. Psalm 119:105

Apply stickers to complete the verse above.

Page 2

Page 6

Page 7

Page 8

Word

Lamp

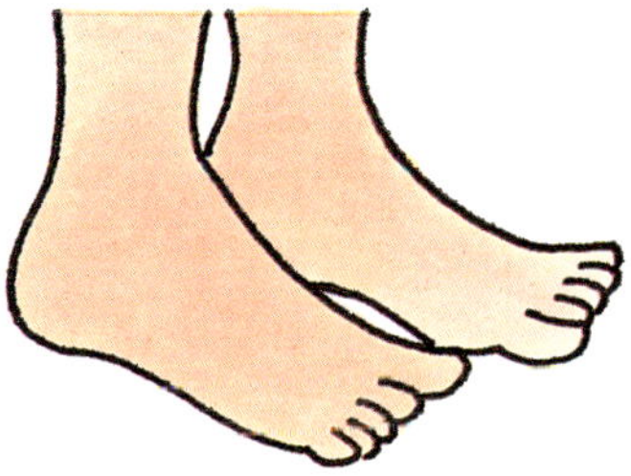

Feet

Light

Path

Page 9

Page 12

Martin Luther

Hans Luther

John Tetzel

Mrs. Cotta

Jesus

God Is with Us Always

Color in the shield next to each picture that shows a time when the Lord helped Luther.

Luther Becomes Knight George

Because Luther did not take back what he said was wrong with the church according to the Bible, the leaders made him an outlaw. Luther hid from them, dressed as a knight, and lived in a castle. Many did not know where Luther was. Use a sticker to change Luther the monk into a knight.

God Is Our Fortress

Words to Remember

God is our refuge and strength. Psalm 46:1

Traditional

(Pronunciation of Latin text is DOH-nuh NO-beese PA-chem.)

Who Am I?

Use stickers and fill in the blanks to tell who is described in the statements below.

1. I was born in Germany.
   I liked to read the Bible.
   I liked to sing.
   I wrote the Ninety-Five Theses.

   ___ ___ ___ ___ ___ ___   ___ ___ ___ ___ ___ ___

2. I worked in a copper mine.
   I took baby Martin to be baptized.
   I carried Martin to school.
   I wanted Martin to become a lawyer.

   ___ ___ ___ ___   ___ ___ ___ ___ ___ ___

3. I was a monk.
   I sold "forgiveness" papers.
   Luther said my papers were wrong.

   ___ ___ ___ ___   ___ ___ ___ ___ ___ ___

4. I liked to hear Martin sing.
   I invited the choirboys to eat with my family.
   I asked Martin to live with us.

   ___ ___ ___   ___ ___ ___ ___ ___

5. I love all people and came to save them.
   I died on the cross to take away your sins.
   I am alive and want you to live in heaven with Me someday.

   ___ ___ ___ ___ ___

Words to Remember

Come, let us sing to the LORD. Psalm 95:1

Tell the Story

Cut out the puppets. Bend the tabs to the back and tape them together. Put the puppets on your fingers. Use them to tell the story of Martin to yourself and to your family and friends.